Lost & Found

First published 2020 by The Hedgehog Poetry Press

Published in the UK by
The Hedgehog Poetry Press
5, Coppack House
Churchill Avenue
Clevedon
BS21 6QW

www.hedgehogpress.co.uk

ISBN: 978-1-913499-60-0

A CIP Catalogue record for this book is available from the British Library.

Lost & Found

by

Vic Pickup

For Si and my family, for their love and support on this journey,

who make each loss bearable, each gain a joy.

Contents

CLEARING OUT

If caught without them, you'd frantically frisk yourself —
cheeks growing ruddy at the realisation
they were on your head all along.

Now you've gone to some unknown place
and it bothers me
that you won't be able to read the signs —
vital, should you reach a crossroads.

Your version of the world was seen through these,
thick plastic and darkly shining —
they're tortoiseshell, I now realise.

I consider the number of evenings we spent searching
for them in time for *The News at Six.*

There's a residue on the arms
above where your ears would have been —
and also the bridge of your nose.
It feels greasy on my fingers;
I rub it in.

Then I sit in your chair wearing them and
everything is out of focus.

How could they go from your most needed possession
to utterly useless —
and what the hell do I do with them now?

STILL LIFE WITH TOYS

The end of a worn-out day and my daughter's dolly eyelids close as soon as she's laid down, her duvet napkin-like to chin.

In the playroom waits a heap of gaudy plastic; cups and saucers, let's-pretend cutlery, a hollow apple, juiceless bunch of grapes.

Felted pastries nuzzle, fuzzed and frayed beside unspreadable yellow butter, gleaming in its dish.

A small wooden spoon lies abandoned, never to be immersed in a hearty broth — instead gripped by a small clammy hand as she stirs the air in her bowl and sings

before summoning me to the carpet, tucking in my bib and waiting for tea to arrive. I chomp and marvel at tiny pine macaroons, PVC sponge cake, knitted strawberries.

Now the pile is losing its glow, nothing to do with the fading light. There won't be many days more when these delicacies are called into play.

Her tea parties will soon be upgraded from teddy bears' picnics to speed dates with Darth Vader and Barbie —

and this lot will be boxed up and left to charity, if they'll take it. Some things, chipped paint flaking, fit only for the bin — for a landfill burial, or blazing in a furnace

somewhere far from here.

MY MOTHER TOLD ME

to live in fear of solitary magpies / dare not repeat Friday night's dream / if a bird
flew into the house / there'd be nothing for it / move out

never put shoes on a table / be in a situation / where there is no escape
but under a ladder

I recoiled at the gifted purse with no coin inside / black cat slinking from right to left
I'd turn around / tempt it back

she had me lopping the ends off bread / smashing through the bottom of an egg
with a spoon / to let the devil out

I winced when someone opened an umbrella indoors / spilled salt / raised a toast
with water / dropped a knife or gave the gift of a blade

if I pointed at the moon / she'd gasp in horror / a broken mirror had me
in tears / I spent days searching / for a good omen / to reverse impending doom

a passer-by would not have known / a pivotal moment / the morning I saw the black
and white bird on a gate / and did not salute it.

SO MUCH WRONG WITH THE WORLD

Slowing, the cold air catches in my throat.
The sky is a grey wash.

There are two dead hares floating,
bloated.

I stop to photograph a bridge of stilts
when she comes bounding over the brow,

lolloping, sweaty, tongue lolling from jaws
like a piece of wet ham. She's meaty, brown

and matted, stumbling off the bridge, down
the ridge, tumbling arse over teat into the water.

All sploshing mutes the distant human pleas
to resist the river.

By the time the owner arrives, puffing,
the panting Lab is neck deep in cold water

with a smile so big all you can do
is get in with her.

WHAT IT MEANT FOR THE WOMEN

They stopped wearing make-up,
didn't bother with the office clobber —
heels pushed to the back of the rack as
flipflops and Crocs came to light.

They became flat-footed, slow treading feet
spreading against the laminate, the stone,
the grass. Some days they didn't brush their hair,
roots reaching up from within, dark and natural.

They immersed themselves in old crafts;
crochet, knitting, watercolour – leaving the phone
to vibrate in another room. They began to read,
knead, blanch, blend, stir, separate and taste.

They planted seeds and couldn't believe their eyes
when a seedling broke the earth; taking delight
as they watched wild birds peck, take flight,
a fresh green tendril in a bright orange beak.

They stood outside in the world and listened
for what seemed like
the first time.

THE DAWNTREADER

The Dawntreader wakes to darkness,
the rectangular glow of time signalling departure.
His boots wait by the door, waxed jacket
hangs stiff above a radiator.

Leaving in stillness, barely a particle
moves at his passing. He reassures the aged collie
with a rough rub down, click of his tongue.

The Dawntreader is the breaker
of dew-threaded webs, the first footprint
in snow. He is the disturber of deer —
they still and hold his eye.

Tinkling the snowdrop bell with a finger,
he bears holly prickle and sticking thistle,
never disapproves of driving rain.

The Dawntreader wades through a mist
that sleeps on the towpath,
pouring onto the canal between rushes,
creeping up the bank in wisps.

He regards the heron perched upon a diving twig,
watching, waiting. A dipped beak
and a glint of silver hangs limp.

The Dawntreader halts atop the railway bridge,
observes the commuters —
grey shoulders reflect grey faces,
coffee cup lids containing their steam.

He walks in the sliver of time between black
and the invasion of day. Wild things go into hiding,
wary eyes watch from beneath the bracken.

The Dawntreader's boots crunch gravel
as he greets the postman, eats his museli,
takes a shirt on a hanger
and goes in his car to work.

THE ART OF PUTTING A FILTER ON LIFE

If you need to see it brighter try Ludwig, pique the senses
with iridescence in Clarendon; make your orange fire, blue
like the sky in your eyes.

Go bold in Juno, amplify the beauty, unreal in X-ProII
then zoom and tell them where to look. Give yourself time
to adjust to the creation you're about to give the world.

Or — if it's too much — if the luminescence screams fakery,
makes your head ache and your vision hurt, recognise
the option to mute. Don't be afraid you'll lose out
in monochrome. Stop yourself from sliding the bar
that makes the contrast greater, watching black
go blacker than it really is.

Instead try Rise, Amero, Crema; soften the edges in Sierra
or Valencia for the old Hollywood glow, vintage cool.
Or — if it's not really you, come back to Normal —

it was more beautiful all along.

SCHOOL FOUNDER'S DAY

June, 2019

Children in Victorian dress
frolic in flecks of sunlight —

they dance and peek
and play hide and seek
between the graves.

I know the residents won't mind —
from beneath the beat
of small feet

I can feel
their rapture.

FRIENDS

There's the one who was here within four minutes
then comes back the morning after with biscuits, thick and chocolatey.

Another, who stood in the doorway, shocked to see me on the floor
whose face is the first I remember.

There's the one who cycled round with a pot plant balanced on each handlebar
jabbed the air with her finger and, quite rightly, put me in my place.

There's the one who posted a card with so much to say
she'd gone over the *Get Well Soon.*

One who told my daughter they love her
when they didn't know I was listening.

There's the one who left banana bread on the mat —
started messages with 'don't reply, just know that'.

There's the one who sent her husband out for baking powder because
I'd run out — and she knows I like to whisk troubles into oblivion.

The one who goes way back and usually lets his wife do the talking
but sent me a kiss at 10pm.

And there's the one who was here, who put me in recovery and did all the right things
and says we'll work it out and tells me five days after to put some make-up on

and brush my hair and he's going to say a word and I might not like it but
resilience

and that is all.

ACKNOWLEDGEMENTS

I'd like to thank to the editors of *Mslexia* and *Runcible Spoon*, where two poems from this pamphlet have been previously published.

I am indebted to poets Anna Saunders, Gill Learner, Robin Thomas and Zannah Kearns for their guidance and support whilst writing these poems. And to Claire Dyer and Jonathan Taylor for much inspiration. Thanks also to my friends at *Thin Raft* and *Inkpot* for their wisdom and encouragement.

My gratitude goes to Charlotte Broster, for helping me find things I had lost without realising, and all those mentioned in 'Friends', who bolstered me in the process.

To Mark Davidson, Editor of Hedgehog Press, for creating what you hold in your hands – I will forever be grateful for this opportunity.